HIDDEN SNARES

OR

Admonitions Addressed to the Young.

A DISCOURSE

OCCASIONED BY PAINFUL EVENTS OF RECENT OCCURENCE, IN THE CITY OF BALTIMORE, AND

Delivered in the Presbyterian Church,

CORNER GREENE AND GERMAN STS.,

APRIL 17TH, 1859.

"Surely in vain the net is spread in the sight of any bird."

BALTIMORE:
PRINTED BY HANZSCHE & CO., 166 BALTIMORE STREET.
1859.

HIDDEN SNARES

OR

Admonitions Addressed to the Young.

A DISCOURSE

OCCASIONED BY PAINFUL EVENTS OF RECENT OCCURENCE, IN THE CITY OF BALTIMORE, AND

Delivered in the Presbyterian Church,

CORNER GREENE AND GERMAN STS.,

APRIL 17TH, 1859.

"Surely in vain the net is spread in the sight of any bird."

BALTIMORE:
PRINTED BY HANZSCHE & CO., 166 BALTIMORE STREET.
1859.

Baltimore, April 19th, 1859.

Rev. H. Dunning:

Dear Sir—The undersigned, young men, members of your church, would respectfully request you to repeat, at such time as you may in your judgment think best, the sermon delivered by you on Sabbath evening last, the 17th inst.

And believing as we do that the truths and warnings it contains may be the means of awakening the thoughtless to reflection, and turning them from the ways of sin into the paths of virtue and true happiness, we also request a copy of it for publication, that it may be placed in the hands of every young man in the church and congregation.

Jos. Hopkins,
John P. Milnor, Jr.,
Jason Rogers,
Wm. F. Rogers,
J. Farris Moore,
T. J. Noyes,
E. T. Cross,
Geo. H. Miller,
Jos. R. Manaca,
Eli B. Beckwith,
Joseph Cowman,
Charles Bayne,
Lewis M. Eastman, M. D.
H. Wm. Eastman,
H. D. Mears,
Geo. G. Knowles

Messrs. Jos. Hopkins,
Jno. P. Milnor, Jr.,
Jason Rogers, and others:

Brethren—According to your request the discourse delivered Sunday night, 17th inst., has been repeated, and I now transmit it as delivered, without time for revision, for any further use you may deem proper to make of it, hoping that the lessons inculcated may not be lost upon the youth of our church and congregation

Very truly yours, in the ministry of Christ,

H. Dunning.

Baltimore, April 29th, 1859.

HIDDEN SNARES.

"*Surely in vain the net is spread in the sight of any bird.*"—PROV. 1, 17.

Our city has recently been the scene of an event of the most painful character. Never before in the history of this commonwealth has such a spectacle been witnessed, and it is most devoutly to be wished that never again may it be. Four unhappy men, charged of wrong doing, having appealed to a jury of their peers, were declared guilty, and adjudged to suffer the extreme penalty of the law. I need not say with what sadness and awe we saw the fatal day approaching. Upon the whole city there fell a most solemn sense of the sacred majesty of law, from the salutary impression of which it is to be hoped it may never recover. Under the solemnity of that approaching day, the followers of evil were arrested in their course, the votaries of pleasure held for a time the half drained cup in an unconscious hand, the children of worldly care hastened less eagerly along the highways of daily activity, and the good of all classes, men and women of faith and prayer, waited incessant supplicants before the throne of Heavenly Grace for their salvation, whose lives were soon to be surrendered at the demand of human law. Of the oppressive solemnity of that appointed morning, as it dawned upon us, I need not speak. First, bright and calm, then overcast, chill and drear, nature seemed to fall into harmony with the sadness of the occasion. As the last hour drew near, the throbbing pulse of this great community languished under the oppression, and as the fatal moment approached when the forfeit was to be paid, men held their breath and the common heart ceased to beat—never rested there upon this community so impressive a sense of the majesty of law and of the inviolability of justice. May the salutary influences of that impression not speedily pass away. We were made to realize how strong is the arm of justice, how sacred her claims, how inviolable her majesty. None was there of us with heart unmoved in behalf of those unfortunate men, and yet who of us would have assumed the responsibility of arresting the demand of law and of exposing society to the consequences of that arrest? If trampled right demanded vindication, if the public weal cried out against red-handed wrong, if the sacred claims of sovereignty demanded defence and justification before the eyes of all, who would have assumed the responsibility of arresting those demands? To him to whose hands alone is committed the power of arrest, they seemed inexorable. The hour came, the demands were met, the claims of law were honored, justice was vindicated, wrong was avenged, the great heart of this community palpitating with sympathy for the wretched, submissively sanctioned what mercy could not reach forth her hand to avert, and, as judgment went forth unto victory, the curtain fell upon a scene which God grant there may never be necessity of repetition in the history of our city.

I would not, my friends, permit such an event to pass unnoticed in the ministrations of the sacred desk. But, while we would recall the scenes of that sad day on this occasion, it is not to harrow your hearts by the reiteration of its horrors. It is not to canvass the guilt or the innocence of those who have already appeared before a higher and an impartial tribunal; not to discuss the question of the propriety of showing or of refusing mercy, even where the claims of justice are confessed; not to inveigh against the course of those who are now beyond equally our sympathy and our blame; not to send a pang through the already lacerated and crushed hearts of those in our community, who have been by their relations to some of those unfortunate men called to drink the bitterest cup of human sorrow, and for whom the whole community has felt the deepest sympathy; not to arraign or condemn, not to praise or blame, not to inculpate or exculpate on any hand, but only, if I may by Divine grace be enabled so to do, to gather up from this painful transaction and send home upon our hearts such salutary *Lessons* as may be fruitful of good through all our life, and especially, if I may be able, to lodge an effectual *Word of Warning* in the heart of the youth yet inexpert of vice and untainted of crime in this my beloved charge. I say I would speak to *the Youth* of this congregation; and am I not called to this by the circumstances in which we are placed? Living, as we do, upon the ground of those tragic deeds which have resulted in this fearful, final catastrophe, in the midst of those haunts where that horrid stimulation was obtained, without whose maddening influence those deeds of blood would not have been done, and seeing many of our youth frequenting such places as can not be visited without stepping upon the precipice of destruction, and knowing their unhappy unconsciousness of their danger, would I not be direlect in duty and worthy of stripes myself not to speak on this occasion, and to remind our young people, who are our pride and our hope, of the lessons and admonitions which their inexperience and natural inadvertence might pass unnoticed? And, my friends, how much the more am I urged to this, as I recall the fact, that those unhappy men, now removed from our midst, were once *Youths* ardent, hopeful, unsuspecting, full of high aspirations and generous impulses as any before me; the tender objects of maternal love and the subjects of parental anxiety as any before me; less predisposed, perhaps, to evil ways and less exposed to temptation than many before me; of whom, perhaps, in the days of their untried innocence none could have apprehended so sad a fall from the ways of virtue and none could have anticipated so sad an end. But they fell; in the midst of life, in the flush of vigorous youth, with all their manly strength still upon them, they fell. A few months ago they could not have looked forward with any personal apprehension of so sad a fate, and perhaps no one living could have thought it possible.

How then,—it is right for that instruction which we wish to derive from these painful events, and pertinent here to our aim to inquire,—*how has this sad catastrophe come about?* what are the agencies, causes, instrumentalities and steps by which it has come to pass?

THE SNARE IS HID.

If we are not mistaken, the Proverb repeated at the head of our discourse will give us the clue that will lead us through all the channel backward and up to the fountain of this overflowing calamity: *"Surely, in vain the net is spread in the sight of any bird."* The concealed power of evil it is and was that has wrought this infinite and irreparable damage to these unhappy young men. In vain indeed, would the net have been spread *in their sight;* in vain would the attempt have been made to allure them into the path that led to so unhappy an end, had that end been visible before them. Nay, my hearers, it was the concealing of the net that ensnared the bird; it was the unseen and unsuspected direction of the pathway that led them onward; it was the circean cup of pleasure that bewitched their senses, and the syren song that allured them until, ere they suspected their danger, they were within the tow of that vortex down which they have whirled and disappeared forever. It is the delusive and pleasurable aspect wherewith evil presents itself to our unfallen youth that gives it its peculiar and often fatal influence over their mind and heart. Let the intoxicating cup be first tendered to your unfallen boy by the bloated hand of the blood stained drunkard, and let it be pressed by words borne upon the foul and foetid breath of the confirmed inebriate, and his purer, natural instincts will revolt the temptation; but let it be presented sparkling with friendship, and wreathed with flowers and smiles by a gentle and lovely maiden, and by hiding the net you will ensnare the bird. In vain will your son be tempted to enter the pathway of revelry and debauch through the door of the low haunts of the vicious and the criminal, but lead him into the gorgeous saloon where the well-dressed company, panoplied in the airs and assurances of fashionable life, throws easy luxuriance over all he sees, and the very magnificence that salutes his eyes, the glare of costly candelabra, the sheen of magnificent mirrors and the dazzling array of fashionable tinselry will effectually conceal from his unsuspicious feet the snare into which he is led. "In vain do you spread the net in the sight of any bird." It is not by exposing vice and crime in their native and naked deformity that you are to seduce our youth into prodigal and vicious ways. It is by concealing their true character under some pleasurable guise that you allure them from the ways of virtue and set them, unawares of the danger, on the road to ultimate ruin.

THE ROAD TO THE SNARE IGNORANTLY ENTERED UPON.

Thus you perceive that the beginning of a ruinous course on the part of a young man is ordinarily *unintentional*; it is not in full view of the nature, the tendencies, the danger, or the consequences of his course; on the contrary, the end is unseen, the snare is concealed, and the victim is caught and held by the powers of evil before he has thought whither he is going. The young man who, under the enticements of youth and beauty, first ventures in the social circle to manipulate the cards, in what he is persuaded is a mere harmless game of whist, least of all suspects that he is taking the first step in the way of his becoming the accomplished, the profane, the hardened, the heartless, the hopeless gambler. And yet, in most cases, there it is, in the social circle at home or among friends, that the downward course is entered upon; there the net is spread, there the bird is snared. The approaches of evil are always hidden, its pleas are always delusive. Tell that noble young man, of generous impulses and high ambitions, encircled by intelligence, beauty and fashion, that these pleasurable hours with cards, dice and wine are the alphabet of a life of debauchery and shame, and he would spurn the insinuation, as did the young courtier of Damascus, when the weeping Prophet foretold his future crimes, "*What! is thy servant a dog, that he should do this thing?*" And yet, *there* is where the evil is begun, where the habit and the power grow upon the unsuspecting victim, and where that fascination fixes upon the soul which cannot afterwards be broken. The young do not generally, foreseeing the consequences, run persistently into evil ways, but under a false and fatal guise are allured and snared ere they are aware of their danger. This is the history of almost all that are ruined in our midst.

THE ADVANCE IMPERCEPTIBLE.

And then, when once they are entered unsuspectingly upon the road to ruin, *how imperceptible and how unappreciated is their advance.* Could they see themselves swimming along upon the current and hastening towards the fatal vortex, with what earnestness would they seek to save themselves! But, like men in a boat loosened from its moorings while they sleep, they glide along, hastening to the precipice in painful unconsciousness of their danger. The advances in decline of character and in wrong doing are always unperceived by him who makes that advance, although it may be painfully manifest to all his friends. Evil doing exercises this blinding and treacherous influence over its agent. Such is its benumbing influence upon the moral feelings, such the perversion it works upon the moral judgment, that he who yields himself to its power least of all will suspect that deterioration it is working in his own character, and least of all suspects the advance he is making in the road to death. That young man whose already vitiated taste seeks gratification in the horrors and startling revelations of flashy police journals, will ere long be found gloating a diseased imagination over the pages of immoral and corrupting books. Then, already conscious of moral contamination, he will not be able to look the virtuous in the face, and advancing in the process of moral degradation, he will be soon found forsaking the company of the virtuous, male and female, and seeking that of the profane, the vicious and the immoral. Entered once upon the downward road, step by step, unconscious of the tendency of his course and of that rapid deterioration of moral character which he is suffering, he hastens along in evil doing, all the while contracting new and more vicious habits, forming new and more vicious intimacies, and forsaking the virtuous of his better days, and, while he thinks himself free and boasts his freedom and capacity of self-control, he is snared and taken. And now, with the loss of others respect he has suffered also the loss of his own, and smitten of conscience, he rushes into new temptations and deeper debaucheries, and swings loose from all restaint, gives the rein to passion, and sweeps down the current, hastening irresistibly to the maelstrom before him. Little does he suspect the advance he has already made; little does he apprehend the whirlpool into which he must almost inevitably plunge. "In vain had you spread the net *in his sight*," but, hidden under the guise of pleasure professedly harmless, he is led onward, is snared, is taken ere he suspects the fatal tendency of his course. He is debauched in mind, in morals, in manners and heart, and is a ruined man before he knows it. He began his career as a youth perhaps in parental disobedience, in Sabbath desecration, in neglect of the house of God, in profanity, tobacco defilement, wine drinking and whist, he ends it in debauchery, in a hopeless corruption of morals, in an untimely breaking down of all his powers, in helpless bondage to depraved habits, in an untimely end, perhaps in a felon's cell, perhaps upon the gallows.

THE SNARE SPRUNG AND THE SUDDEN SURPRISE.

There is, moreover, involved in this idea of the text, not only the delusive and hidden character of the evil wherewith the young are enticed, not only their unintentional departure from virtuous ways when first yielding to temptation, and not only their unappreciated advance from step to step when once they have fallen, but also *the suddenness of their surprise* when the snare is sprung and the victim is caught. The young man swung loose from virtuous restraint will be allured from step to step in his downward course, will advance from vice to vice, from crime to crime, hardening under the depraving influence of evil associations, unconscious of the deterioration that has already taken place in his moral character, and flattering himself that all is well until some last, fatal step is taken, perhaps in a drunken brawl, or under some peculiar temptation or provocation, some one outbreaking act springs the snare and he is caught. Debauchery ends in ruin, vice demands its penalty, crime demands its punishment, and dishonor, a prison's cell or the gallows awaits him who "despised counsel and rejected reproof." And how great will be his surprise when for the first, he realizes that his whole past course led only to that snare into which he is now fallen and in the meshes of which he is fatally entangled. Then, when too late, will he take up the lamentation, "*How have I hated instruction and despised reproof.*"

And do we not see all this illustrated in the unhappy history of these four young men whose untimely end all must deplore? When first they entered upon that course which has terminated so sadly, little did they think whither it tended and where, if pursued, it must inevitably end. When by their first profane oath they gave the first shock to their conscience and to their friends, when they first began to visit the drinking saloon and the club room, when they entered the pathway of her allurements, whose "steps take hold on hell," when they turned away from the quiet delights of home, from the Sabbath, from the sanctuary, when they consorted with the idle, the dissolute, the profane, the immoral, little did they think, not at all could they be persuaded, that they were entering the doorway to destruction; and little do the young men that are now by the same doorway, entering the same pathway think—not at all will they believe, that like danger and ruin are before them. They see not the snare, and, being in their own conceit, "wiser than seven men that can render a reason," they press on, and if not prevented by a timely arrest, debauchery, dishonor and irretrievable ruin await them. When the snare shall have been sprung upon them, then will they first realize what is the character of that course they have pursued. You, young man, that have already and so skillfully acquired that horrid art of profanity, you that dwell with depraved delight upon the pages of demoralizing books, you that have already listened to the solicitations of passion, to the vile enchantments of the hag of hell whose steps lead to the dead, that seek your associations in the saloon and the club-room, and have forsaken those pure and elevating female circles where most you should delight to seek society, you now little think, you will not now believe whither tends and where ends that path into which you have entered. Be admonished in time. Let our text admonish you that the snare which is certainly laid in your pathway will as certainly be hid from your eyes. You may not see the danger, others do; they already see whither your feet are tending and already have serious alarm in your behalf. It would, perhaps, surprise young men in this congregation if they were told of the serious apprehensions of their best friends in their behalf. Already have some of you entered the road to ruin, and though it may provoke a smile or a sneer to tell you so, yet, let me say, that how far you have advanced is much more definitely known than you at all suspect. Stop, young man, stop! your course will lead to inevitable dishonor, exposure, ruin. "In vain were the snare laid, if laid in your sight." Look at the issue of that career on which you are entered and turn your feet to the paths of virtue and peace ere it be too late. Be admonished by a friend, even also that friend in your own bosom, whose voice you have so long disregarded, be admonished and stop ere you set foot into the fatal snare and you are caught and held inextricably. "*Surely in vain is the net spread in the sight of any bird.*"

My friends, *my young friends, and you that are parents,* we must not permit these lamentable events of recent occurrence in the history of our city to pass unnoticed and unimproved. There is a voice, yea, there are many voices which speak to us from our streets, from the silent cells of our prisons, from the unhonored stage so recently erected in our midst, which must not utter their warnings unheeded. The young should heed them for they admonish where danger lies. Parents should heed them, for if future victims there are to be, some of our families are to supply them; the gray hairs of perhaps some of these fathers and mothers must come down with sorrow to the grave. It is shocking to see a parent indifferent to the course, character and conduct of the young. Nobody is so vulnerable as a parent—none has his happiness so completely in other's keeping. A son, a daughter by a single act may wreck that happiness for this world. An unthoughtful, a careless, a reckless parent is a monstrosity in nature, to be feared and shunned.

ADMONITORY LESSONS.

And, my friends, by these recent occurrences how earnestly are we admonished that *Sabbath desecration* is one of the first steps that lead the young to ruin. "*When at twelve years of age I forsook the Sabbath school, I entered upon that course which has ruined me,*" said one of those unhappy young men. The youth who turns his back upon the Sabbath school, the House of God and the family altar, has already set foot in that road that leads to ruin. Happy will it be for him if, perceiving the danger, he retraces his steps before it is too late. Painful were the scenes which, on our return from the fulfilment of an appointment to preach in the environs of the city this afternoon, we witnessed. Beer-drinking, ball-playing, horse-trotting and fighting, were the pastimes with which men desecrated the hours of God's Holy Day, and the majority too of the actors in these scenes were of the young. Surely the testimony of recent events should be a sufficient admonition upon this point.

And with what earnest warning do recent confessions speak to us all in regard to *the use of the intoxicating cup.* Twelve men, it is said, were recently tenants of our prison cells, charged, and six of them convicted, of capital crime, committed during the past year, and all of them are reported to have perpetrated the deed while under the influence of strong drink, and in some cases it is said, that that drink, without whose poisonous stimulation the deed could not have been done, was dealt out to the agents who accomplished the work by those who pursue their nefarious traffic in our own neighborhood, Oh, sad indeed will be their account, who for gain, dealt out the liquid poison that maddened the brain, that nerved the arm and stimulated the purpose, that struck down the lamented Rigdon. Them, that under the influence of that drink, struck the blow, you have put out of the world. And what do you with those who for money administered the maddening potion? For a part of that money paid in gold into your city treasury, you license them to deal out again, and thus prepare at your hands other agents for future crimes, and other subjects for future spectacles like that which a few days since, drew so large a concourse to the outskirts of our city. Young man, the intoxicating cup has wrought this ruin; these Satanic pest-houses have stimulated to these deeds of blood; be admonished; shun the cup and shun those gateways to perdition as you would the plague, as you would death itself. Remember, the danger that exists will not show itself, for "*Surely in vain is the net spread in the sight of any bird.*"

And how emphatic is that voice which now admonishes us of the *dangerous influence of bad company*. When began those young men to walk that road that has led to so untimely an end? They began when they forsook the society of home, of brothers, sisters, parents, friends, and sought that of the idle, the dissolute, the profane, the vicious, when they left the family circle for the club-room and the drinking saloon; when they left the Sabbath school and the sanctuary for those places where vice and crime do haunt, and for those companionships whose words are poison, whose touch is pollution, and whose influence is death. One of those young men, in a final letter to his former companions, said:—"*Liquor and bad associations are the bane which has ruined others as well as me; and oh! let me entreat you to remember the fate which has followed my transgressions and profit by it.*"

Another said, "*Avoid evil company, as to this, more than any other circumstance, is to be attributed my lamentable end.* * * * * *Avoid intemperance*—follow some lawful and legitimate pursuit in life, and seek for happiness where alone it can be found, in serving God."

Had they but adhered to the associates of their virtuous days, they might now be filling honorable positions in society, respected and honored by all, but forsaking the virtuous and the good and consorting with the idle and the vagabond, that which the wise man long since prophesied has again come true in them: "*The companion of fools shall be destroyed.*"

My young friends, suffer from your pastor an earnest admonition and a kind entreaty.—Let me admonish you that dangers beset your pathway on every side; let me entreat you as you value your purity of morals, your good name, your character, your standing in society; as you value your prospects for success, for usefulness, for happiness in life; as you value health of mind and body, of heart and soul; as you value any good here, and hope for any hereafter, avoid and refuse the companionship of the idle, of the dissolute, of the profane, of those that desecrate the sabbath day, that despise the holy solemnities of the House of God, and turn away from the society of the pure and the good.—Listen not to their language, it will contaminate; heed not their advice, it will cause to err, yield not to their solicitations, they will lead astray; follow not their example, it tends to ruin; fear not their wrath, it cannot harm. Hear ye, the admonition of the wisest of men.

"My son, if sinners entice thee consent thou not;" "Cease to hear the instruction that causeth thee to err;" "Enter not into the path of the wicked and go not in the way of evil men. Avoid it, pass not by it, turn from it and pass away, for they sleep not except they have done mischief, and their sleep is taken away unless they cause some to fall; for they eat the bread of wickedness and drink the wine of violence." "My son, take fasthold of instruction, keep her, let her not go, for she is thy life." "*If thou be wise, thou must be wise for thyself; if thou scornest thou alone shalt bear it.*"

My young friends, let a pastor, who wishes your highest welfare, entreat you. Be wise, resist temptation; "flee youthful lusts, which war against the soul and drown many in perdition." Already some of you stand upon a precipice. Oh, be wise; turn your feet from evil ways; seek ye "wisdom's ways;" her ways are "pleasantness; seek ye her "paths," they are "peace."

God forbid that any of you should be written among that unhappy number who involve their family in dishonor, themselves in ruin and "*bring down the gray hairs of their parents, with sorrow to the grave.*"

www.ingramcontent.com/pod-product-compliance
Lightning Source LLC
LaVergne TN
LVHW020637110826
845149LV00004B/1241
* 9 7 8 1 4 1 8 1 9 1 2 0 7 *